FEB 02 2017

Science Fair Projects About the Sun and the Moon

Robert Gardner

Enslow Publishing
101 W. 23rd Street
Suite 240
New York, NY 10011
USA

enslow.com

Published in 2017 by Enslow Publishing, LLC.
101 W. 23rd Street, Suite 240, New York, NY 10011

Library of Congress Cataloging-in-Publication Data

Names: Gardner, Robert, 1929-
Title: Science fair projects about the sun and the moon / Robert Gardner.
Description: New York, NY : Enslow Publishing, 2017. | Series: Hands-on science |
Audience: Age 8-up. | Audience: Grade 4 to 6. | Includes bibliographical references and index.
Identifiers: LCCN 2016019995| ISBN 9780766082175 (library bound) | ISBN 9780766082151 (pbk.) | ISBN 9780766082168 (6-pack)
Subjects: LCSH: Sun—Juvenile literature. | Moon—Juvenile literature.
Classification: LCC QB521.5 .G3687 2017 | DDC 523.7078—dc23
LC record available at https://lccn.loc.gov/2016019995

Printed in China

To Our Readers: We have done our best to make sure all website addresses in this book were active and appropriate when we went to press. However, the author and the publisher have no control over and assume no liability for the material available on those websites or on any websites they may link to. Any comments or suggestions can be sent by e-mail to customerservice@enslow.com.

Portions of this book originally appeared in the book *Far-Out Science Projects About Earth's Sun and Moon* by Robert Gardner.

Illustrations by Joseph Hill.

Contents

Introduction

The sun and Earth are very far apart from each other—93 million miles (150 million kilometers)! Yet they are joined by a special force, gravity. The sun's gravity makes Earth move around the sun. We say Earth orbits the sun. How lucky for us! The sun gives us the light and heat we need to live.

In the same way, Earth's gravity makes the moon move around us. Sometimes you see a bright moon at night. Other times, even if the sky is clear, you can't see the moon at night. You will find out why as you do the experiments in this book. You will also learn a lot more about both the sun and the moon.

Entering a Science Fair

Most of the experiments in this book have ideas for science fair projects. However, judges at science fairs like experiments that are creative, so do not simply copy an experiment from this book. Pick one of the ideas and develop a project of your own. Choose something you really like and want to know more about. It will be more interesting to you. And it can lead to a creative experiment that you plan and carry out.

Before entering a science fair, read one or more of the books listed under Further Reading. They will give you helpful hints and lots of useful information about science fairs.

Safety First

To do experiments safely always follow these rules:

1 Never look at the sun. It can cause permanent damage to your eyes!

2 Always do experiments **under adult supervision**.

3 Read all instructions carefully. If you have questions, **check with the adult**.

4 Be serious when experimenting. Fooling around can be dangerous to you and to others.

5 Keep the area where you work clean and organized. When you have finished, clean up and put all of your materials away.

6 Use only alcohol thermometers. Some thermometers contain liquid mercury. It is dangerous to touch or breathe mercury vapors. Mercury thermometers have been banned in many states. If you have a mercury thermometer in your house, **ask an adult** if it can be taken to a local mercury thermometer exchange location.

1

Using the Sun for Direction

Things You Will Need:

- an adult
- clear weather
- 2 wooden stakes
- hammer
- open level place where sun shines all day
- stick or Popsicle sticks
- yardstick or tape measure
- watch or clock

How can you use the sun to find out which way is north? Write down your ideas and your reasons for them.

Ask an adult to help you with this experiment. And remember, do not look directly at the sun! It can damage your eyes!

1 On a sunny morning, hammer a stake into the ground. Choose a place that is level and will be in the sun all day. Be sure the stake is straight up and down.

2 A bit before midday (11 a.m. to 1 p.m.) begin marking the end of the stake's shadow every 5 or 10 minutes. You can use a stick to make a scratch mark, or you can mark the positions with Popsicle sticks. Keep doing this until you can see that the shadow is getting longer.

3 Use a yardstick or tape measure to find the length of the shadows you marked. Find the mark where the stake's shadow was shortest. That shadow pointed north. Hammer a second stake into the ground on that mark.

4 How can you find east and west? Leave the stakes in the ground for more experiments.

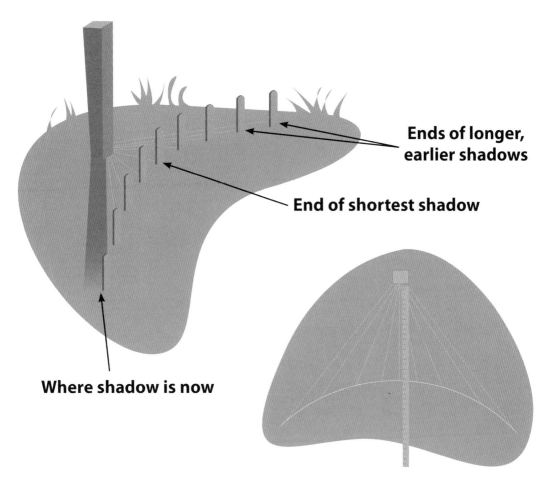

Ends of longer, earlier shadows

End of shortest shadow

Where shadow is now

Measuring the shortest shadow

Using the Sun for Direction: The Facts

The sun reaches its highest point in the sky at midday. It casts the shortest shadows at that time. Midday (the time halfway between sunrise and sunset) may not be at noon. At midday, the sun is directly above a point south of you. It casts a shadow that points north.

To find east and west, stand in front of the first stake. Face north. Raise your arms straight out. Your right arm will point to the east. Your left arm will point to the west.

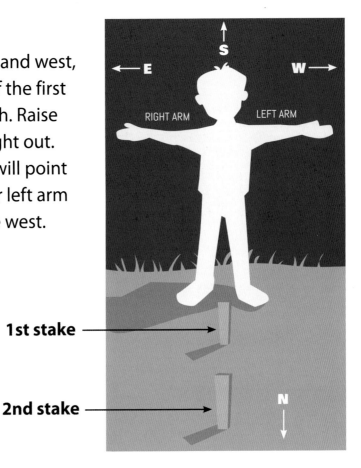

1st stake

2nd stake

Ideas for Your Science Fair

- Does midday where you live always happen at the same time? Do experiments to find out.
- Use a globe and a soda straw to find out where the sun is directly overhead at midday.

2

Seasons and the Sun

Things You Will Need:

- clock or watch
- stakes from Experiment 1 to find true east
- paper and pencil
- calendar

It will take a year to do Experiments 2 and 3, but you can learn a lot from them. While doing these two experiments, you can do Experiments 4 through 10.

As you will see, the sun follows a path across the sky. Do you think its path will begin (sunrise) and end (sunset) in the same places as the seasons change? Write down your ideas and your reasons for them.

1 Get up in time to see the sun rise. Use the stakes from Experiment 1 to find east. Standing between those stakes, note the direction of sunrise. Do not look directly into the sun!

2 Draw a diagram like the one shown. On your diagram, write something to help you remember where the sun rose. You might write, "Just left of the Smith's garage," "Behind our big maple tree," or something like that. Don't forget to date your diagram. Did the sun rise north of east? South of east? Or true east (in line with your location of east in Experiment 1)?

3 Do the same thing from the same place at sunset.

4 Continue to mark the direction to sunrise and sunset at least once a month for a year. Be sure you always stand on the same spot, between the same two stakes. What changes do you think you will see?

Seasons and the Sun: *The Facts*

As you have probably discovered, the sun does not always rise in the same place. It does not always set in the same place either. In the northern hemisphere, from spring through

May 1st

The sun rose just to the right of our maple tree.

Sunset was behind the Williams's garage.

direction to sunset

summer, the sun rises and sets north of east. In the fall and winter, it rises and sets south of east. A true east sunrise and a true west sunset happen only twice a year. Those dates are the first day of spring (around March 21) and the first day of fall (around September 21). On those two days, the sun shines directly on Earth's equator.

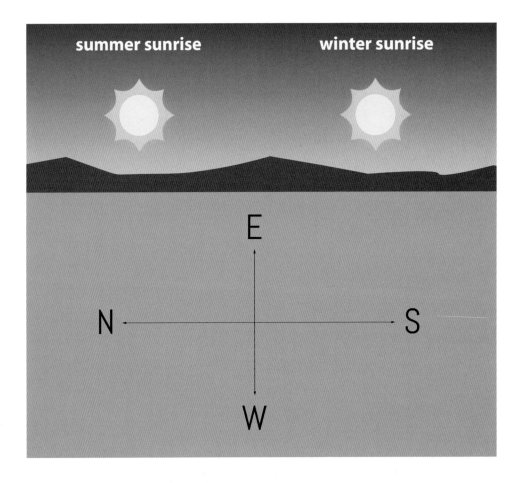

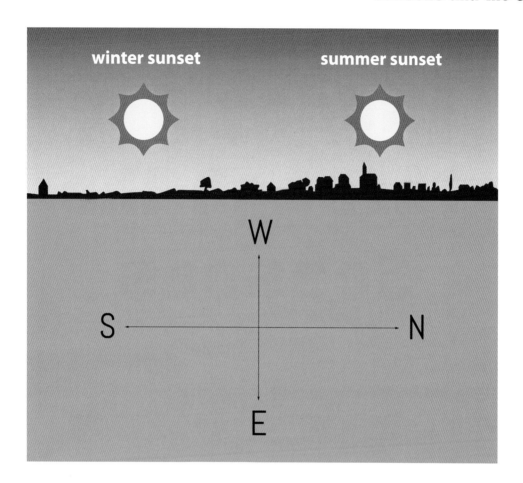

winter sunset

summer sunset

W

S — N

E

Ideas for Your Science Fair

- Use shadows to show the direction of sunrise and sunset.

- Record the time of sunrise and the time of sunset as seasons pass. How can you explain these time changes?

3

Midday Sun Through the Seasons

Things You Will Need:

- pencil
- clay
- sheet of paper
- dark room
- flashlight

- stake from Experiment 1
- yardstick
- pencil
- notebook

How does the height of the sun's path across the sky change as seasons pass? Write down your ideas and your reasons for them.

Let's Investigate!

Shadows can be used to compare the height of any light, including the sun. You can do an experiment to see that this is true.

1 Stick a pencil upright in a small lump of clay. Put the pencil and clay on a sheet of paper on the floor.

2 Turn out the lights so the room is dark.

3 Shine a flashlight on the pencil. Watch its shadow as you move the flashlight higher. Watch its shadow as you lower the flashlight. When is the shadow longest? When is it shortest?

4 Go to the first stake you put in the ground during Experiment 1. Mark the ends of its shadows around midday. Write down the length of its shortest (midday) shadow in a notebook.

5 Continue to measure its shortest midday shadow at different times of the year. What do your measurements tell you about the sun's height during its path across the sky? How does the height of its path change as the seasons pass?

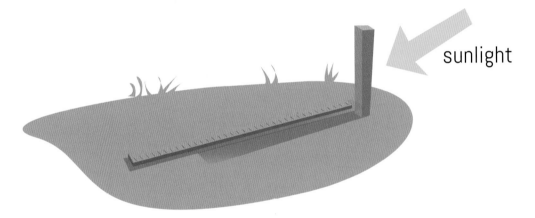

sunlight

Midday Sun Through the Seasons: The Facts

As you found, the pencil's shadow grew longer when the flashlight was held lower. The shadow grew shorter as you shined the light from a higher place.

The same is true of shadows cast by the sun. A midday summer sun casts short shadows. The midday winter sun's shadows are much longer. The path of a summer sun is high and long. The path of a winter sun is shorter and lower. Compare the time for the sun to travel across summer and winter skies. Which path takes longer?

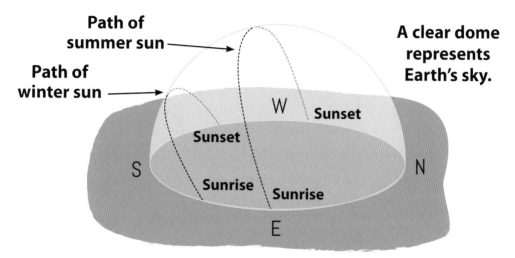

Ideas for Your Science Fair

- Use a clear plastic dome to represent the sky. Figure out a way to map the sun's path across the sky on the dome.

- On a sunny day, how does the length and direction of your shadow change? Can you explain the changes you see?

4

Using the Sun to Tell Time

Things You Will Need:

- board at least 12 in (30 cm) on each side
- tape
- sheet of paper
- hammer
- finishing nail 2–3 in (5–8 cm) long
- sunny, level place outdoors
- chalk
- pencil
- watch or clock

How can you use the sun to make a clock? Write down or draw your ideas and your reasons for them.

Let's Investigate!

1 Find a board at least 12 inches (30 centimeters) square. Tape a sheet of paper to the board. Hammer a finishing nail a short way into the board. The nail should be upright and near one end of the board as shown.

2 Put the board on a sunny, level place outdoors shortly after sunrise. The nail should be on the south end of the board.

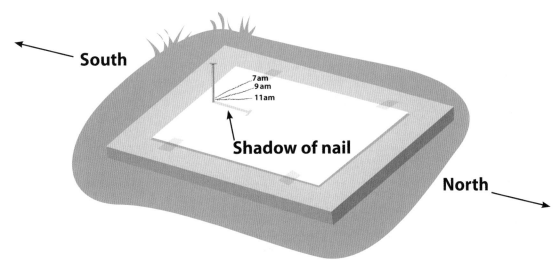

South

7am
9am
11am

Shadow of nail

North

3 Use a pencil to mark the nail's shadow on the paper. Do this every hour until sunset. Label each shadow you mark with the time you read on a watch or clock.

4 Use chalk or some other way to mark the outline of the board on the ground so you can put it back in the same place later.

5 After several days, compare the times on your sun clock with the times on your watch or clock. Do the times still agree? Do they agree after a week? After a month? After several months?

Using the Sun to Tell Time: *The Facts*

Early Egyptians used a sun clock like the one you made. As you found, the sun clock is not very accurate. Its time did not agree with your watch or clock time for long. One reason is that Earth's orbit around the sun is an ellipse.

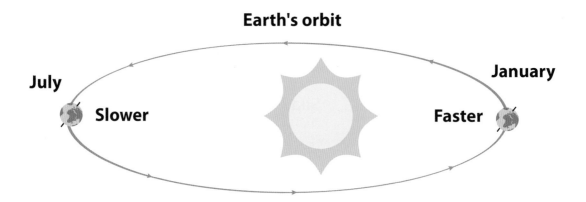

Earth's orbit

July

Slower

January

Faster

Analemma

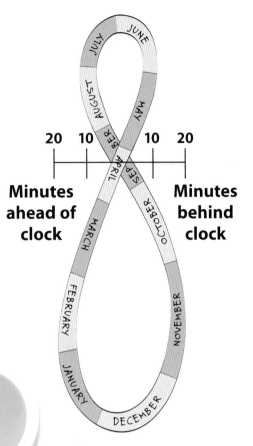

20 10   10 20

Minutes ahead of clock

Minutes behind clock

An ellipse is an oval shape. In January, when Earth is closest to the sun, it moves faster along its orbit. In July, when it is farther from the sun, it moves slower.

On a globe you will find an analemma. It looks like a long thin number 8. It shows how much sun time is ahead or behind a clock's time each day of the year.

Ideas for Your Science Fair

- **Build a sundial using a gnomon. The angle (steepness) of the gnomon should match your latitude. Is it a more accurate timer than the sun clock you made?**

- **Figure out a way to use your watch and the sun to find the approximate direction of true south.**

5

The Sun's Heat

Things You Will Need:

- 2 aluminum pie pans
- flat black paint
- masking tape
- 2 outdoor alcohol thermometers
- 2 clear plastic bags
- twist ties (if needed to seal bags)
- cardboard box
- window in bright sunlight
- clock or watch

Do you think a black surface will take in more of the sun's heat than a silver one? Write down your ideas and your reasons for them.

Let's Investigate!

1 Get two aluminum pie pans. Paint the inside of one pan with flat black paint. Let the paint dry.

2 Use masking tape to attach an outdoor alcohol thermometer to the inside of each pan. (See the drawing.) Be sure the tape covers the thermometer bulbs.

3 Put each pan inside a clear plastic bag. Seal the bags.

4 Put both pans in a cardboard box. Put the box near a window in bright sunlight so that the sun shines directly on both pawns.

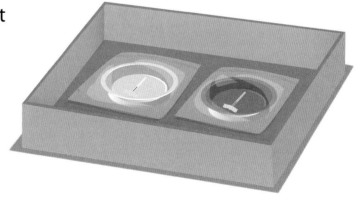

5 Look at the thermometers every 5 minutes. Does the air temperature inside the pans increase? If it does, in which pan does the air get warmer?

6 Take the pans out of the sunlight before the temperature gets to 100 degrees Fahrenheit (40 degrees Celsius).

The Sun's Heat: *The Facts*

Have you ever stood in the bright sun wearing dark clothes? If you have, you may have noticed how warm you felt.

Dark surfaces absorb (take in) more heat from the sun than lighter ones. Lighter surfaces, such as a shiny aluminum pie pan, reflect a lot of the sunlight. The heat in that sunlight is not absorbed. As a result, light-colored things do not get as warm as darker ones.

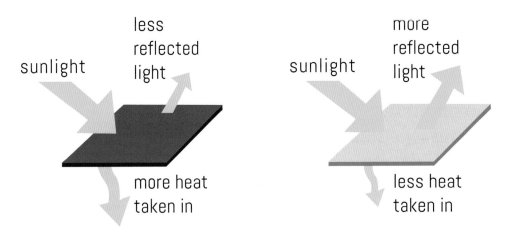

Lots of sunlight is absorbed as heat.   **Lots of sunlight is reflected.**

6

Sunlight's Colors

Things You Will Need:

- bright sunshine
- garden hose with spray nozzle
- cloudy day
- prism
- white wall
- lightbulb

Do you think you can find colors in sunlight? Write down your ideas and your reasons for them.

Let's Investigate!

1 Stand with your back to the sun. Use a garden hose with a nozzle to spray a fine mist into the air. The spray should be in front of you as shown in the drawing. What colors do you see? You have made a rainbow. The rainbow shows you all the colors that are in sunlight.

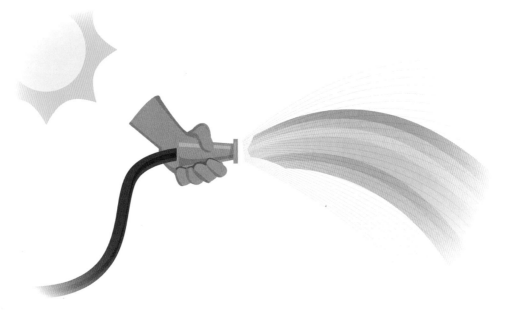

2 Repeat the experiment on a cloudy day when the sun is not shining. Can you see a rainbow? What does this tell you?

3 Here's another way to see what colors are hidden in the sun's light. Hold a prism in sunlight. Hold it near a white wall. Turn the prism until you see a band of colors on the wall.

4 Hold the prism near a white surface several feet from a glowing lightbulb. Can you separate the light from the bulb into colors?

Sunlight's Colors: *The Facts*

A prism can separate ordinary white light into colors. It does this by bending the light. Some colors, such as violet, bend more than others, such as red. The bending makes the white light break apart into all the colors you see in a rainbow.

Raindrops, or water drops sprayed from a hose, act like tiny prisms. They reflect the light and bend it. The bending causes the colors to separate. The reflection sends the colored light back to your eye.

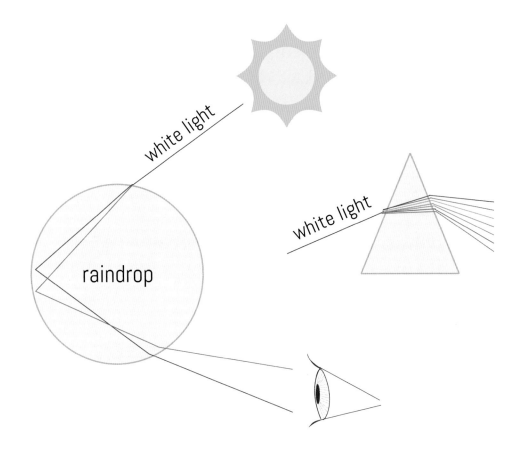

Ideas for Your Science Fair

- Can moonlight cause a rainbow?
- Look for and try to explain other colors you may see in the sky.

7

Phases of the Moon

Things You Will Need:

- pen or pencil and a notebook
- local newspaper

Does the moon always look the same? If not, does it change from day to day? Write down your ideas and your reasons for them.

Let's Investigate!

1 Find your newspaper's weather section. It will tell you the date of a new moon.

2 A day or two after a new moon, look for the moon in the west as the sun sets. What does the moon look like? It is called a crescent moon.

3 Look for the moon each day. Draw pictures of the moon so you will remember its shape. Be sure to look for the moon at sunset. How does its shape change as days pass? How does it appear to move farther from the sun? Where do you see the sun when you see a full moon rising?

4 Because of cloudy weather, you may not see the moon every day. But keep looking for the moon as days and months pass.

5 After you see a full moon, begin looking for the moon early in the morning. How does its shape change as days pass? How much time separates one new moon from the next? Why can't you see a new moon?

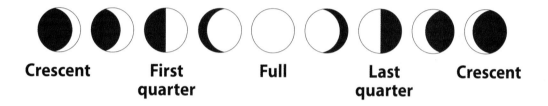

Crescent   First quarter   Full   Last quarter   Crescent

Phases of the Moon: *The Facts*

There are 29 ½ days between new moons. The same time passes between full moons.

You saw a thin crescent moon near the setting sun. The moon grew fatter as it moved farther from the sun in the sky every night. When a full moon is rising, the sun on the opposite side of the sky is setting. After a full moon, you can see the moon in the morning. It shrinks as it slowly moves closer to the sun in the sky. Finally, it becomes a crescent on its other side as it rises shortly before the sun. A new moon can't be seen. You will learn why when you do the next experiment.

Ideas for Your Science Fair

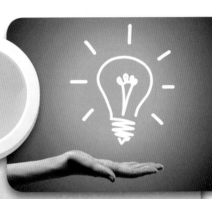

- Does the moon always rise in the same place? Does it always set in the same place?

- Why can we sometimes see the moon in the daytime? Why are we sometimes unable to see the moon—even on a clear night?

A Model of the Moon

Things You Will Need:

- white Styrofoam ball, white golf ball, or Ping-Pong ball
- long pin or nail or some clay and a stick
- dark room
- incandescent, frosted lightbulb
- stool

Why does the moon's appearance change? Write down your ideas and your reasons for them.

1. Put a white Styrofoam ball on the sharp end of a long pin or a nail. (You can also use a white golf ball or a Ping-Pong ball supported by some clay on the end of a stick.) The white ball represents the moon.

2. Do this experiment in a dark room. Turn on one incandescent, frosted lightbulb. The lightbulb represents the sun. Sit on a stool several feet from the lightbulb. Hold the ball above your head. Your head represents Earth.

3. Slowly turn around on the stool, moving to your left. Watch the ball as you turn. Notice how the lighted (brighter) part of the ball changes. (The darker part of the ball will not be totally dark. Walls and ceiling reflect some light onto the ball). When do you see a crescent moon? A first quarter? A full moon? A last quarter? Another crescent? A new moon?

How does this model help you explain why the appearance of the moon changes? Keep your moon model for Experiment 10.

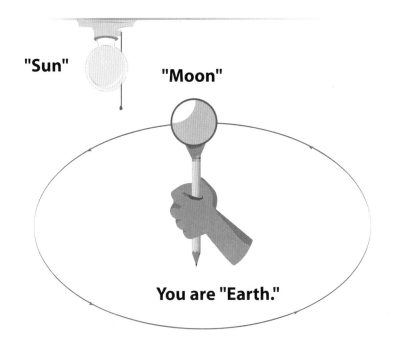

"Sun"

"Moon"

You are "Earth."

A Model of the Moon: *The Facts*

As the moon circles around (orbits) Earth, it reflects different amounts of sunlight back to Earth. When it is between Earth and the sun (a new moon), we can't see it. All its reflected light goes back toward the sun. When it is on the side of Earth opposite the sun, we see a full moon. Then the whole side of the moon facing Earth reflects light to us. Between new and full moons, we see different amounts of the moon. You saw how this works as you turned on the stool.

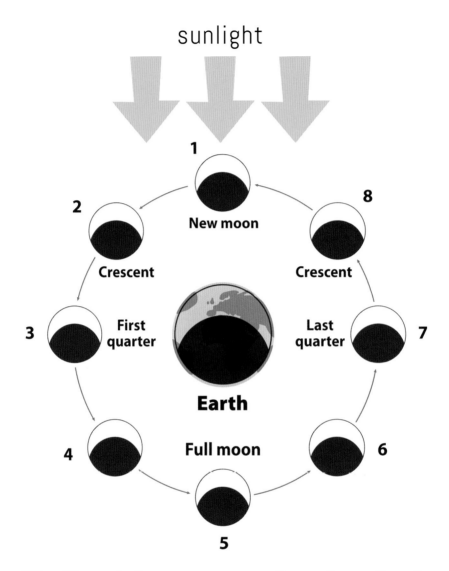

sunlight

1
New moon

2
Crescent

8
Crescent

3
First quarter

Last quarter
7

Earth

4

Full moon

6

5

The Moon's Appearance as Seen from Earth

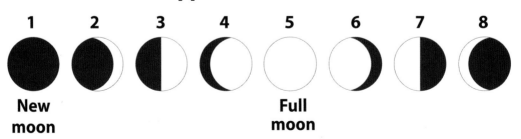

1 2 3 4 5 6 7 8

New moon

Full moon

9

Observing the Moon's Surface

Things You Will Need:

- good binoculars or a telescope

How will the moon look different if you look at it through binoculars or a telescope? Write down your ideas and your reasons for them.

Let's Investigate!

1 Pick a clear night when the moon can be seen. Look at the moon through binoculars or a telescope. Does it look the same as it did when seen with just your eyes? If not, how is it different?

2 Look at the moon through binoculars or a telescope when it is at or near first quarter. Notice the shadows you can see on the moon. What do you think causes the shadows? Where are the shadows longest? Where are they shortest? Why are some shadows longer than others?

Observing the Moon's Surface: The Facts

Seen through binoculars, the moon is not smooth. It has many "scars" (craters) where meteoroids have hit its surface.

Sunlight makes shadows on the moon just as it does on Earth. The higher the sun, as seen from the moon, the shorter the shadows. The lower the sun, as seen from the moon, the longer the shadows. If you were standing near long shadows on the moon, the sun would be rising or setting. If the shadows were short, the sun would be higher.

Ideas for Your Science Fair

- Look at a full moon when it is rising over the eastern horizon. Then look at it later when it is high in the sky. When does it look larger? Design an experiment to show that its size does not change.
- Try to explain why the moon looks larger as it rises.

10

Solar and Lunar Eclipses

Things You Will Need:

- scissors
- drinking straw
- penny or dime
- frosted lightbulb
- large ball, such as a soccer ball
- moon model from Experiment 8

Sometimes all or part of the sun or moon becomes dark. This is called an eclipse. What causes an eclipse? Write down your ideas and your reasons for them.

Suppose the moon got directly on a line between Earth and the sun. What would happen? (Usually, a new moon is slightly above or below a straight line between Earth and the sun.)

Let's Investigate!

1 Use scissors to make a slit in the end of a drinking straw. Put a penny or a dime in the slit.

2 Let a bright, frosted lightbulb represent the sun. The coin represents the moon. Close one eye. Hold the coin close to the other eye. Move the coin between your eye and the lightbulb. How much of the bulb is covered? How much of it can you see?

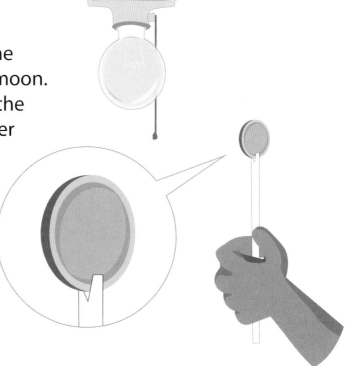

3 Move the coin closer to and farther from your eye. Where is the coin when it covers the whole lightbulb? Part of the lightbulb?

4 What happens when the moon blocks the sun from sight? Hold your moon model from Experiment 8 between the lightbulb (sun) and a larger ball (Earth). Look for the smaller ball's (moon's) shadow on the larger ball (Earth). If you were in the shadow, what would happen to your view of the sun?

Solar and Lunar Eclipses: The Facts

Once in a while, the moon passes directly between the sun and Earth. This is called a solar eclipse. When it happens, the moon's shadow falls on Earth. If you are in the dark part of the shadow (see the drawing), the whole sun disappears. If you are in the lighter part of the shadow, part of the sun disappears. Never look at the sun during an eclipse.

When Earth is directly between the sun and the moon, Earth's shadow falls on the moon. This is called a lunar eclipse, but the moon doesn't disappear. Some sunlight that is bent by Earth's air reaches the moon. This gives the moon a reddish color during a lunar eclipse. It is safe to observe lunar eclipses.

Total Solar Eclipse (eclipse of sun)

Moon's shadow
falls on Earth

View
of sun

Before

During

After
total
solar
eclipse

Moon

Earth

Sun

Total Lunar Eclipse (eclipse of moon)

Sun

Moon moving
around Earth

Glossary

lunar eclipse A lunar eclipse happens when Earth is directly between the moon and the sun. Then Earth's shadow falls on the moon, and we see the moon grow dark.

meteoroids Small objects moving through space that sometimes hit planets and moons. The moon's many craters were made by meteoroids that struck its surface.

midday The time halfway between sunrise and sunset when the sun is highest in the sky.

new moon A new moon is when the moon is between Earth and the sun. A new moon cannot be seen from Earth because all the sunlight hitting the moon is reflected away from Earth.

prism A wedge-shaped piece of glass or plastic object that can bend light, separating white light into all the colors it contains.

rainbow A semicircle of colors from red to violet made when sunlight is reflected and bent by raindrops. From an airplane you can sometimes see a full circle of colors.

shadow An area where light is blocked by an object.

solar eclipse A solar eclipse occurs when the moon is directly between Earth and the sun. Then the moon's shadow falls on Earth. Within the shadow, all or part of the sun is blocked from view.

Further Reading

Books

Ardley, Neil. *101 Great Science Experiments.* New York: DK Ltd., 2014.

Buczynski, Sandy. *Designing a Winning Science Fair Project.* Ann Arbor, MI: Cherry Lake Publishing, 2014.

Dickmann, Nancy. *Exploring Planet Earth and the Moon.* New York: Rosen Publishing's Rosen Central, 2016.

Latta, Sara. *All About Earth: Exploring the Planet with Science Projects.* North Mankato, MN: Capstone Press, 2016.

McGill, Jordan. *Earth Science Fair Projects.* New York: AV² by Weigl, 2012.

Sohn, Emily. *Experiments in Earth Science and Weather.* North Mankato, MN: Capstone Press, 2016.

Websites

NASA

climatekids.nasa.gov

NASA's **Climate Kids: NASA's Eyes on the Earth** *is filled with links and games about air, weather, water, energy, plants, and animals.*

NASA Star Child

starchild.gsfc.nasa.gov

Learn more about the sun and the moon.

The Nine Planets

nineplanets.org

Take a tour of the solar system. Then click on Sun or Moon for even more details.

Index